2/97

TUBERCULOSIS

TUBERCULOSIS

Elaine Landau

A Venture Book
Franklin Watts
New York Chicago London Toronto Sydney

Photographs copyright ©: National Library of Medicine: pp. 11, 20, 24, 26, 50, 71, 73; Library of Congress: pp. 16, 18, 28; National Jewish Center for Immunology and Respiratory Medicine: pp. 31, 41, 51; Ben Klaffke: pp. 36, 37, 38, 57, 67, 69, 77, 80.

Library of Congress Cataloging-in-Publication Data

Landau, Elaine.
Tuberculosis / by Elaine Landau.
p. cm. — (A Venture book)
Includes bibliographical references and index.
ISBN 0-531-12555-6
1. Tuberculosis. (1. Tuberculosis. 2. Diseases.) I. Title. II. Series: Venture book (Franklin Watts, Inc.)
RC311.L334 1995
616.9'95—dc20 94-39305 CIP AC

Printed in the United States of America
6 5 4 3 2 1

CONTENTS

TUBERCULOSIS

1

TUBERCULOSIS

DATELINE TANZANIA

Wilson Kwanyan was frightened. He'd been sick for some time, and the severe cough, fever, and achiness he experienced persisted. Kwanyan saw a local healer, who assured him that his illness resulted from a curse his uncle had put on him. The two men were involved in a land dispute, which was never amicably settled. Shortly afterward, Kwanyan's uncle had left the village. He'd recently returned as a very ill man and had died several months later. Now Wilson Kwanyan wondered if he would share the same fate.

To secure adequate medical care, Kwanyan had to travel to Naamanga, a town in the country's north. As he was too ill to embark on the journey alone, his father and friends fashioned a stretcher out of tree branches for him. With their assistance, the ailing man managed to reach the town's health clinic.

At about the same time, Chen Li, a woman from northern Hunan, China, was experiencing many of the same symptoms as Wilson Kwanyan. Her health problems first began about two years earlier when she'd had a bad cough and had begun losing weight. After she started spitting up blood, the middle-aged woman finally went to the village doctor.

The medication prescribed for her (a combination of injections and pills) absorbed nearly all of her husband's modest income. Realizing the situation's gravity, however, the couple paid the doctor and hoped Chen Li would recover soon. Within a few weeks, the woman's worst symptoms subsided, and she even put on some weight. The doctor stressed to Chen Li and her husband that she must continue treatment, but by then the couple's savings had been used up. Although they could have borrowed money for the medication, they decided against going into debt. Instead both remained grateful for Chen Li's improvement and prayed it would continue.

After a few months, however, her health began to deteriorate. Often Chen Li coughed up blood or shivered in bed while trying to keep warm. Although the village was just down the hill, she rarely went there any longer because even that short trip left her breathless and exhausted. Chen Li tried her best to cope with her debilitating symptoms, but then something happened that caused her concern. Her only grandson, who lived with the couple, became sick as well. The small boy lost weight and often had coughing fits. At that point, his grandmother realized that her decision to discontinue her medication had affected someone other than herself.

The cough that plagued Chen Li and her grandson had also become a problem for a man named Tom Smith, who largely lived on the streets of London. There was little stability in Smith's life. A homeless alcoholic, he tried to find shelter in abandoned buildings on the colder nights as he struggled to survive. When Smith's cough worsened, there were few resources available to him. Once, after being taken in by the police, Smith spent the entire night coughing in his jail cell. The next day, the authorities made him see a doctor, who warned Smith to return for further help. But the homeless man resumed his medication only when he was brought into custody on vagrancy charges.

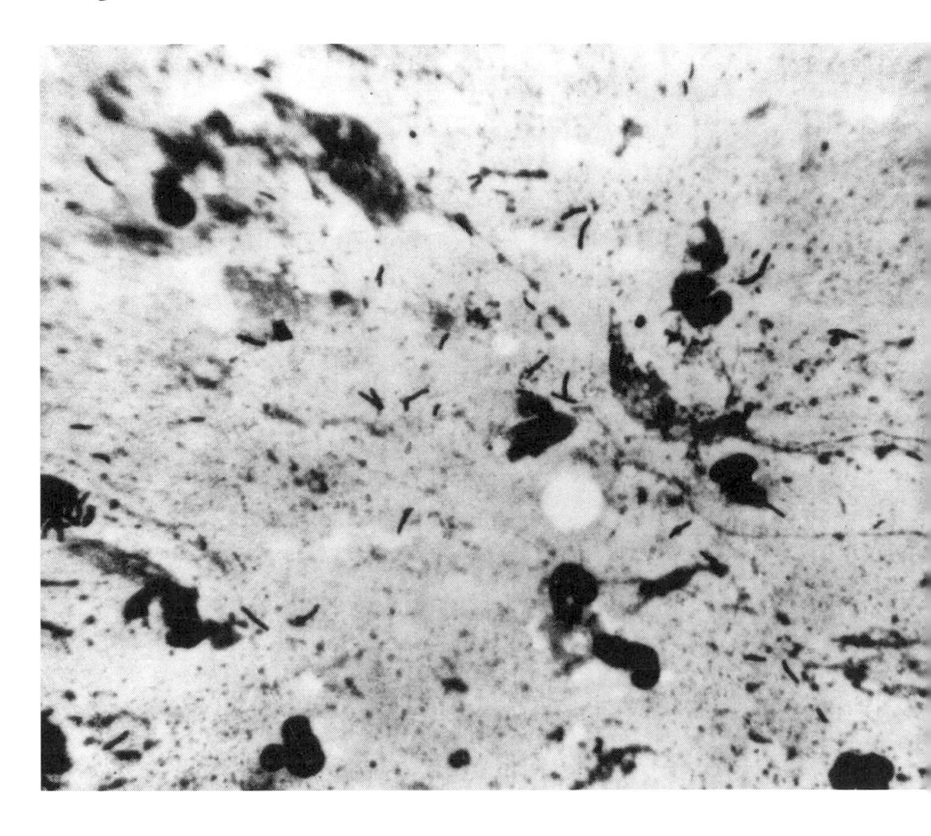

This specimen seen under a microscope shows red corpuscles and the rod-shaped bacterium responsible for tuberculosis.

This situation continued as Smith's condition worsened. After several years, Smith finally agreed to enter a hospital. Perhaps he wanted a warm bed, or maybe he knew he was a danger to others, but in any case Smith remained hospitalized for eight months while he continued to receive uninterrupted treatment.

Across the Atlantic Ocean in the United States, for the first time in years, significant numbers of people were also beginning to experience the same symptoms as Wilson Kwanyan, Chen Li, and Tom Smith. At first, they were particularly evident in crowded prisons, homeless shelters, and poor urban areas—but there was little doubt among medical professionals that the illness was spreading. Soon, there were reported cases among prison personnel and health care workers as well as scattered incidents in middle-class suburbs.

All were suffering from a disease known as tuberculosis, or TB. Although TB had been largely eradicated in the United States, as of 1985 it had come back and was rapidly spreading. By 1990, there was a 16 percent rise in tuberculosis, and many urban areas had TB rates five to seven times higher than the national average of 10 cases per 10,000 people. In some of the most deprived sectors of America, TB rates were even higher than in the poorest nations on earth.[1] Unfortunately, a deadly killer had returned.

2

IN THE BEGINNING

Tuberculosis is an ancient deadly disease that dates back to nearly the beginning of time. Evidence of the illness was found in the remains of a young man who died in 4,000 B.C., during the Stone Age. TB has also been recognized in Egyptian mummies, as well as depicted in paintings on the walls of their tombs. By the seventeenth century, London death certificates indicated that at least one in five deaths in the city was a result of the disease. But soon those numbers would be considered small. Between the seventeenth and nineteenth centuries, tuberculosis swept through England as well as the rest of Europe in epidemic proportions and was often referred to as the "white plague."

As the disease simultaneously raged in America, many assumed it was brought to the Western Hemisphere by European settlers, as were smallpox, measles, mumps, and chicken pox. This wasn't true, however, in the case of tuberculosis. Archaeologists, studying the remains of American Indians, note that the peoples of both North and South America suffered from tuber-
losis long before Europeans ever landed on t

By the turn of the nineteenth century, it's estimated that the international tuberculosis death rate had risen to approximately seven million people a year. Hardest hit were the industrialized, urban centers, with New York and London heading the list. Approximately half of the world's population had come in contact with TB, and many unknowingly harbored the still inactive germ in their lungs. Toward the end of the nineteenth century, there was even growing speculation that the continuing epidemic might eventually result in the end of European civilization and culture.

As tuberculosis continued to wreak its havoc, doctors on both sides of the Atlantic helplessly stood by, unable to curb it. Early remedies were useless in curing the illness and in some cases even placed the victim in greater jeopardy. The ancient Romans suggested TB cures that included eating the flesh of a female donkey in a broth. Another popular remedy involved swallowing "the ashes of sine-dung mixed in raisin wine."[1]

To the disappointment of TB victims and their families, the situation hardly improved with time. In England during the 1820s young ladies with tuberculosis, or consumption as the disease was often called, were urged to rub sulfuric acid on their chests after breathing in warm air. Twenty years later, an ineffective but highly priced brown sugar solution became a popular TB cure. In the 1880s, a potentially lethal but nevertheless sought-after remedy came into vogue. It largely consisted of a mildly poisonous hallucinogenic substance that had been mixed with alcohol, strychnine, chloroform, and morphine.

As there was little doctors could do to help their patients, a TB diagnosis became the equivalent of a death sentence. Yet, because the disease initially appeared to affect Europe's wealthy upper class, tuberculosis was almost considered a fashionable way to die.

The pale, wasting-away look of TB victims was generally associated with spirituality, refinement, and pureness of heart. As the famous English poet Lord Byron said in 1828, "I look pale, I should like to die of consumption [TB]. . . The ladies would all say 'Look at that poor Byron, how interesting he looks in dying.'"[2] Another popular writer of the time underscored Byron's assessment of the stylish disease, when he wrote, "[In the early 1820s] it was all the fashion to suffer from chest complaints; everyone was consumptive, poets especially: it was good form to die before reaching the age of thirty."[3]

The disease's chicness, however, quickly faded with the advent of the Industrial Revolution. During this period, large numbers of overworked and poorly nourished workers toiled long hours in crowded, damp, poorly ventilated buildings. TB became rampant among this population and was soon regarded as a poor person's disease.

Yet regardless of whether the illness was deemed a "stylish sickness" or the "scourge of the masses," the medical community had still not discovered a way to control it. Most people believed that TB sprang from an inborn weakness—if you were destined to get it, falling victim to the disease was inevitable. Although the French surgeon Jean-Antoine Villemin proved in 1865 that TB was contagious, his results weren't taken seriously. Instead, the first truly significant scientific breakthrough in conquering tuberculosis occurred nearly thirty years later. It took place at a meeting of the Berlin Physiological Society in March 1882, when a German physician named Robert Koch from the Hartz Mountains addressed the group regarding his research.

Koch's remarkable results left his audience speechless. Through a series of experiments, the doctor had

On a sweltering night in New York City, TB sufferers living in crowded, poorly ventilated tenements take to the streets for a breath of fresh air.

isolated a rod-shaped bacterium he called tubercle bacillus (known as *Mycobacterium tuberculosis* today), which he had found in the lesions of both humans and animals suffering from the disease. After cultivating the bacilli in his lab, Koch produced the illness in animals he inoculated with it. Shattering the myth of TB as an inborn inevitability, the German doctor had identified the cause of the world's most devastating disease.

Robert Koch's findings were a major turning point in the fight against TB. The public was thrilled when, just eight years later, the respected physician came out with another exciting announcement. This time, Koch claimed to have perfected a cure for TB—although he was somewhat evasive in specifying precisely what that cure was. Under public pressure, however, he later admitted that it largely consisted of a simple extract of the tubercle bacilli.

Anxious to save themselves, hordes of TB patients flocked to Germany for treatment. In the city of Berlin alone, more than two thousand TB patients began taking Koch's remedy. But the results were extremely disappointing. Instead of improving, the patients began to die at an even faster rate than those who had received no treatment at all. It was soon obvious that the man who had found the microorganism responsible for TB had not found a cure for the disease. The situation further deteriorated when it was learned that the German government made a secret pact with the physician to promote and sell his "cure" and split the profits.

Meanwhile, others in the medical profession undertook the search for a cure. An assortment of serums were generated by researchers who had used goats, cattle, rabbits, monkeys, and guinea pigs to produce their vaccines. But nothing worked, which left TB victims as desperate as ever. Many resorted to the host of quack cures offered by charlatans who promised imme-

German physician Robert Koch gained fame as the doctor who identified the microorganism responsible for TB.

diate relief as well as renewed vigor. Sadly, at times these measures worsened the patient's condition or even resulted in painful deaths.

Because doctors had long advocated the benefits of a healthful climate, numerous TB sufferers in the United States decided to flee the harsh winters and humid summers that they were used to. Thousands relocated to warm, dry southwestern states. While this migration was a commercial boom to developing towns and cities in the region, there was no evidence that TB victims were helped in any way.

The spread of tuberculosis also gave rise to a new type of health-care institution known as sanitoriums, which meant "a place to heal" in Latin. Although these facilities were technically not hospitals, they were soon filled with tuberculosis victims hoping to be cured. The first substantial TB sanitorium in the United States was established in 1854 in Saranac Lake, New York, by a young physician named Edward Livingston Trudeau. Trudeau, who had suffered from tuberculosis himself, felt his health had improved after spending some time in the clean air environment of the Adirondack Mountains. He described how the refreshing surroundings initially lifted his spirits as follows:

> *During the entire journey (to the Adirondacks) I had felt a gloomy foreboding as to the hopelessness of my case, but, under the magic influence of the surroundings I had longed for, these all disappeared and I felt convinced I was going to recover.*[4]

In later describing his progress, he added:

> *[L]ittle by little, while lying out under the great trees, looking out on the lake all day, my fever stopped and my strength slowly began to return.*[5]

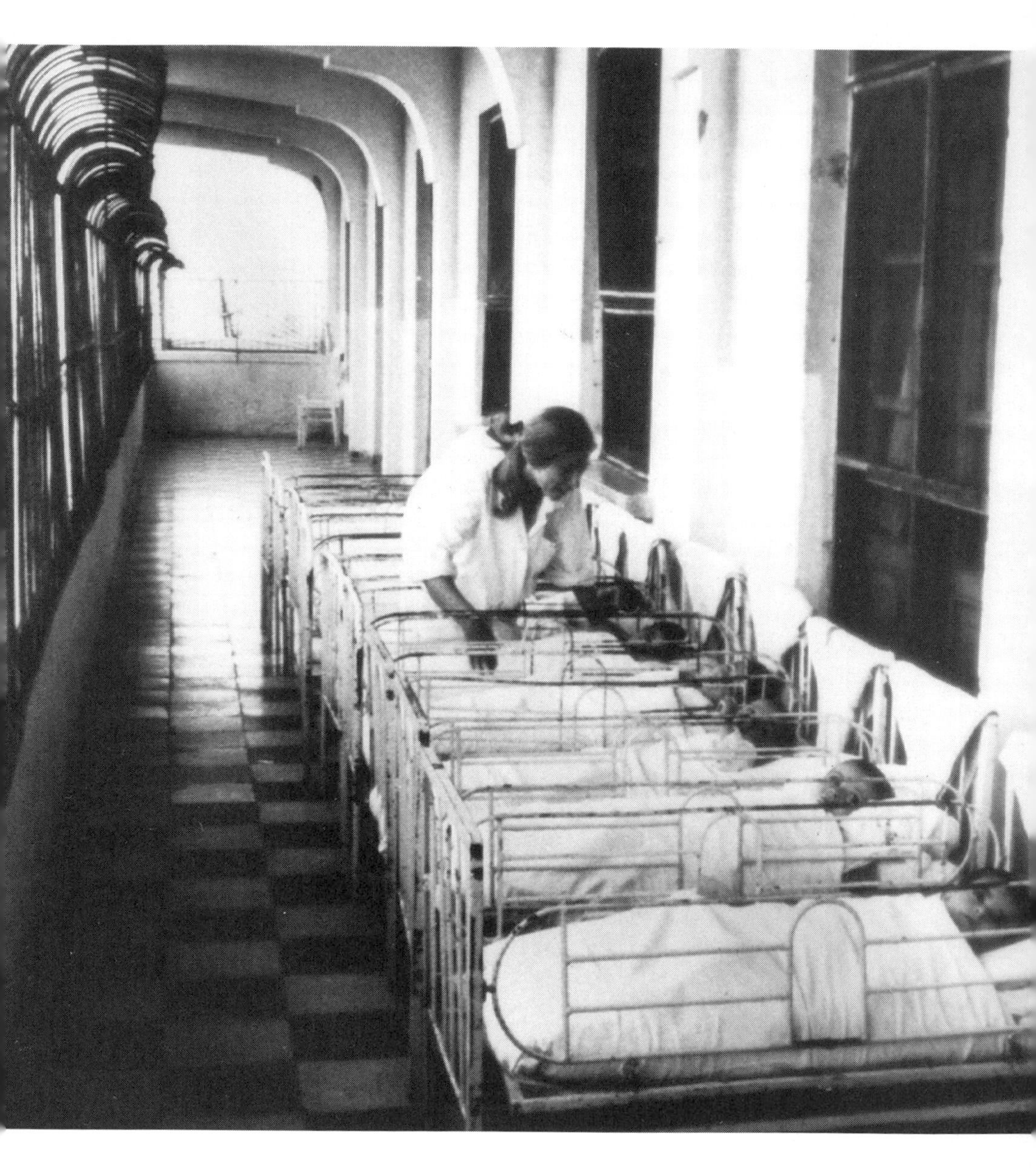

Small children with tuberculosis rest at a sanatorium.

Actually the sanitorium cure was largely based on false assumptions. At the time, many people wrongly believed that TB damaged the body when a weak or sluggish heart failed to pump the disease's poison from the lungs. Sanitorium advocates believed the thin mountain air would force the heart to work harder, thereby enabling it to ward off the illness.

The recuperation process at sanitoriums entailed clean mountain air, a balance of rest and exercise, and a healthful diet. These institutions were more like small communities of sick people than traditional medical centers. There were usually separate work and recreation areas, a library and a chapel, as well as specially designated sections for bedridden patients. Those well enough to do so could learn woodworking, leather work, brass work, or frame making. There were also ample opportunities to exercise and read.

Sanitorium life was characterized by the vast number of rules and regulations that patients were required to follow. Daily activities tended to be highly regimented: residents were told when to rise and when to sleep, what to eat, how to cover their mouths properly when coughing, how much time should be spent in the outdoor air, even how to bathe and brush their teeth. Above all, patients were encouraged to be optimistic about their condition. Under no circumstances was the topic of death to be discussed.

Between 1910 and 1940, hundreds of sanitoriums were filled with TB patients hoping to be cured. In reflecting on these novel institutions, some social critics argue that their extensive regulations were merely the medical profession's attempt to exert some control over an uncontrollable disease that would eventually consume their patients.

At sanatoriums, fresh air, sunshine, and high altitude were considered essential for recovery. In this photograph, TB-stricken young people play outdoors after building a snowman.

There is also considerable doubt as to whether sanitoriums were of any genuine help. Although these facilities were widespread, they only accommodated a small fraction of the millions of tuberculosis victims. Not wanting to fail, they also did not accept people at the more advanced stages of the disease. This meant rejecting the most contagious patients, who ideally should have been quarantined there. Generally, the poor were left to die at home with their families, while those who had just been diagnosed and had ample funds for medical care filled the nation's sanitoriums. In the final analysis, sanitoriums may have made little difference to either TB victims or to society at large. Records indicate that sanitorium patients died at the same rate as those who remained at home.

Meanwhile, the fight to conquer TB continued on other fronts. More than half a century after Dr. Robert Koch's discovery of the microorganism causing the disease, researchers still hadn't perfected a cure. Because treatments to eliminate TB weren't effective, medical professionals and social reformers tried to emphasize preventing its spread. Of course, some backing this effort were more concerned with their own welfare than with that of the general public. Many in affluent neighborhoods were conscious of the TB-ridden slums that were too close for comfort. They worried that their cooks, maids, and butlers who had become an intricate part of their lifestyle might bring the disease into their own realm.

These fears, coupled with the genuine desire of some physicians and reformers to alleviate suffering, gave rise to the War on Consumption. The essence of his "war," as it was referred to, was a high-geared, informational campaign aimed at the American public. Employing every avenue of mass communication available at the time, the message reached its audience through radio, newspapers, motion pictures, and pamphlets. The goal was to both encourage good health habits and raise the moral standards of low-income, working-class people. Yet in making their point, statewide action groups were often smugly condescending to the poor. For example, the Texas Anti-Tuberculosis Society ran the following "public-service" announcement in the *Dallas News*:

Funds for the War on Consumption were partially raised through the sale of Christmas seals as shown here.

DON'T SPIT on the floor of your shop.
WHEN YOU SPIT, spit in the gutters or in a spittoon.
Have your own spittoons half full of water, and clean them out at least once a day with hot water.
DON'T COUGH without holding a handkerchief or your hand over your mouth.
DON'T live in rooms where there is no fresh air.
DON'T work in rooms where there is no fresh air.
DON'T sleep in rooms where there is no fresh air.
Keep at least one window open in your bedroom day and night.
Fresh air helps kill the consumption germ.
Fresh air helps to keep you strong and healthy.
DON'T eat with soiled hands—wash them first.
DON'T DRINK WHISKEY, beer, or other intoxicating drinks; they will do you no good, but will make it harder for you to get well.
DON'T SLEEP IN THE SAME BED with anyone else, and, if possible, not in the same room.[6]

Unfortunately, at times hostility toward poor and minority-group members suffering from TB was overwhelming. This was made especially clear in the remarks of the well-known anti-TB crusader Ellen La Motte, when she noted, "[It] is primarily and essentially a disease of the poor. . . . People of this class are by nature weak, shiftless, and lacking in initiative and perseverance. They have neither inherited nor acquired moral strength . . . and are often vicious besides."[7]

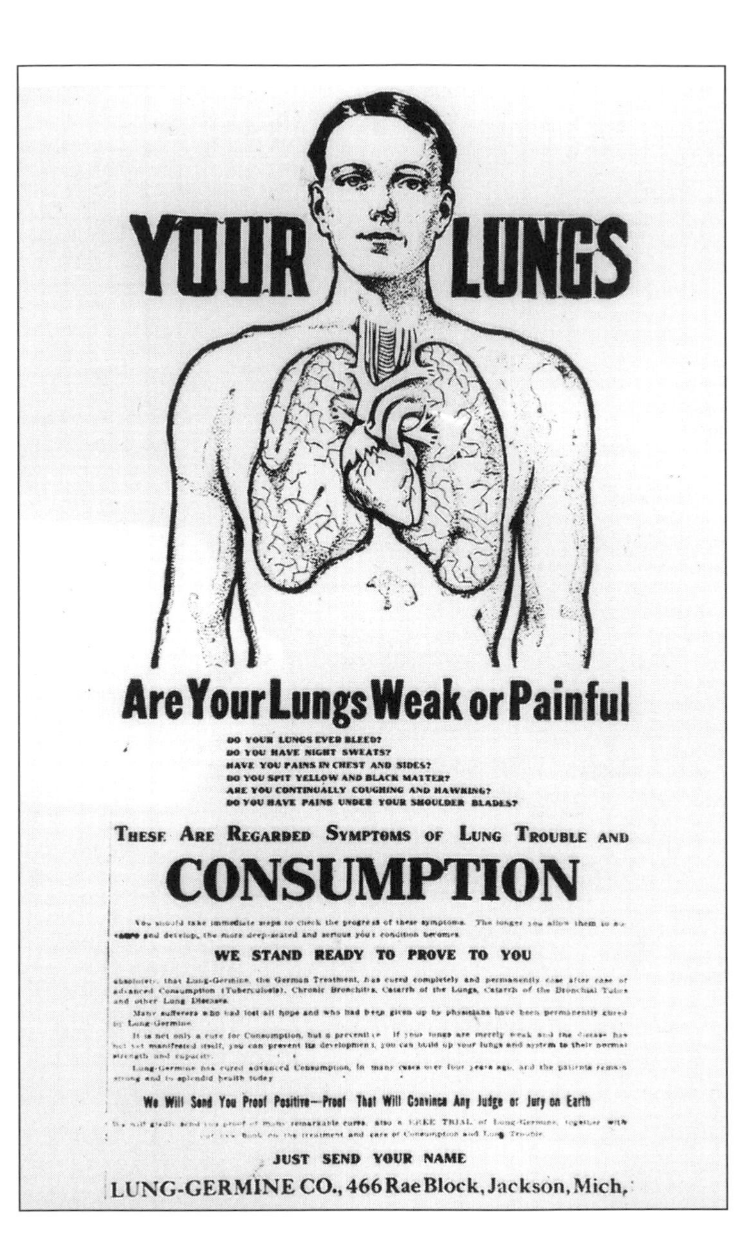

This poster showing a man's heart and lungs was part of the widespread campaign to inform the public of the symptoms and dangers of TB.

With the passage of time, TB victims, or lungers, as they were sometimes negatively referred to, came to be viewed as a blight on society. This perceived threat to the population's overall well-being was a factor in drawing state and local government representatives into the War on Consumption. Among the public officials who became well known in this arena was Herman M. Biggs, New York City's Board of Health general medical officer.

Biggs launched a tireless crusade to eliminate TB from New York as well as the rest of the country. He actively worked to institute cattle inspections, because drinking contaminated milk from TB-infected cows had become a major source of disease transmission. The pasteurization of milk was another method for reducing the risk of TB from cows. Biggs skillfully used the media to stress the contagious nature of the illness and emphasized the importance of disinfecting rooms that had been used by those with active TB. He made hospitals keep TB patients in isolated wards, and also required public health care facilities to forward the names and addresses of tuberculosis patients to the health department.

These measures, however, were just the start of Biggs's intensive city sweep. He pushed through municipal regulations requiring mandatory registration of all TB patients within city limits. Those refusing treatment were forcibly sent to municipally run centers where they were medicated and isolated. Many of the most serious cases were shipped to a harshly run facility under the auspices of the Department of Charities and Correction on a mile-and-a-half strip of land in the East River known as Blackwell's Island.

Critics of these schemes argued that the government had no right to invade and control the lives of individuals whose only crime was to have become ill.

New York City's Board of Health general medical officer Herman M. Biggs was accused of violating the civil liberties of TB victims by forcibly detaining and treating those who refused voluntary medical care.

But Biggs refused to back down, asserting that strong measures were crucial to protect the public. As he noted in 1897, when addressing a meeting of the British Medical Association in Montreal, Canada:

> *The government of the United States is democratic, and the functions performed by sanitary authorities paternal in character. We are prepared, when necessary, to introduce and enforce, and the people are ready to accept, measures which might seem radical and arbitrary, if they were not plainly designed for the public good, and evidently beneficent in their efforts. Even among the most ignorant of our foreign born population, few or no indications of resentment are exhibited to the exercise of arbitrary powers in sanitary matters. The public press will approve, the people are prepared to support, and the courts sustain, any intelligent procedures which are evidently directed to the preservation of the public health."*[8]

At one point, Biggs's "no nonsense" treatment of poverty-stricken tuberculosis victims degenerated into what became known as his "work cure." Any destitute TB sufferer, who could stand or even sit up, was put to work while remaining isolated from the public. As a spokesperson explained the program's rationale, "These were individuals whose lives were so worthless to the community, that it would be an unpardonable waste of public funds to give them the benefit of the sanitorium cure."[9]

Biggs was able to garner support for his dubious measures because much of America harbored deep and irrational fears regarding TB. While a person is most likely to get tuberculosis after repeated close contact with someone in the late stages of the disease, many people didn't even want to pass a TB victim on the street. Those suspected of having the disease often lost their jobs or apartments. Barbers refused to shave TB-stricken customers, and many store owners made them unwelcome in their establishments. The U.S. immigration service even prohibited foreigners with visible signs of the disease from entering the country.

While these tactics were enforced throughout America, the medical profession continued its search for a TB cure. In 1908, researchers came up with a skin patch test that revealed if a person had already been exposed to the TB bacterium. A further development the following year allowed physicians to identify an active case of TB through testing of the patient's sputum (mucus usually mixed with saliva, which has been coughed up from the respiratory tract). While such diagnostic tools were useful, countless people were still left clamoring for a cure.

This prompted doctors to resort to crude and often extremely painful measures in tackling the disease. Some tuberculosis patients underwent an agonizing surgical procedure, known as pneumothorax, in which one of their lungs was surgically collapsed. Even though pneumothorax was rarely effective, the operation was not abandoned until the mid-1950s. Still another, even more excruciating, option performed on TB patients was thoracoplasty. This process entailed removing some of the patient's ribs—in numerous cases, ten or more ribs might be taken out at a time.

In 1943, however, an important medical breakthrough occurred. A drug called streptomycin was found to be effective in combating tuberculosis. At first, the medication looked promising: chest X rays of the vast majority of patients taking streptomycin showed a dramatic clearing of their lungs, compared to only 8 percent of sanitorium patients who hadn't

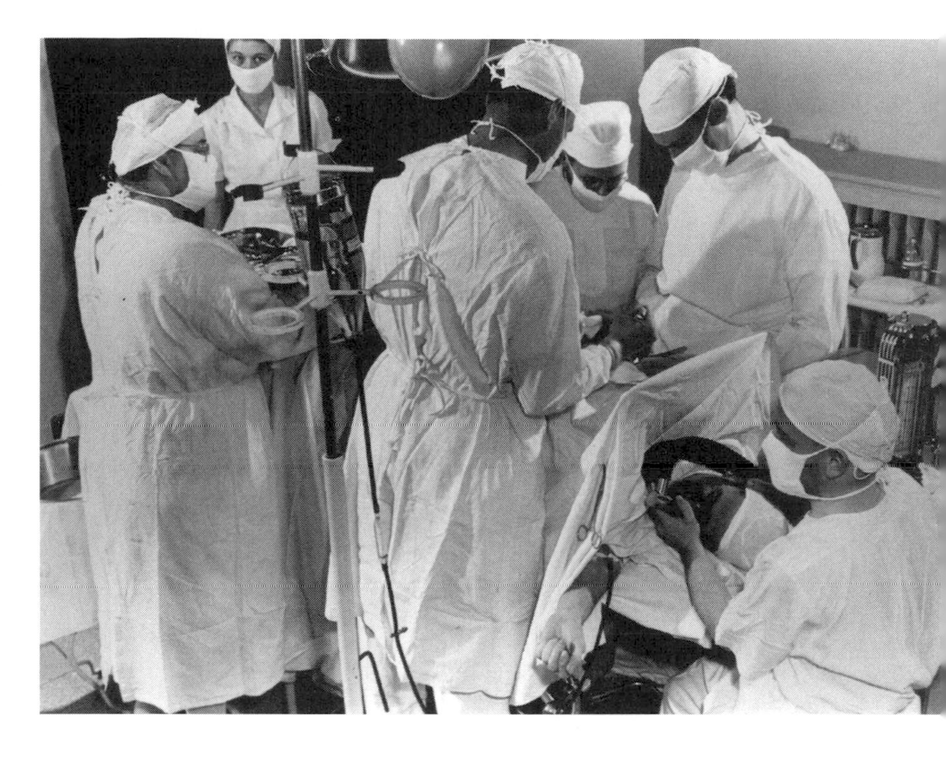

Doctors surgically collapse a TB patient's lung to halt the disease's progress.

taken any medication. Within a subsequent six-month period, only four of the sanitorium patients on streptomycin died, as opposed to fourteen patients who were not taking the medication.

Optimism over the wonder drug faded, however, when another group of physicians analyzed the same group of patients five years later. As might be expected, thirty-five of fifty-two sanitorium patients who had not been administered streptomycin had died. But, surprisingly, thirty-two out of fifty-five patients who had received the drug had died as well. It was clear that in many instances streptomycin only temporarily reduced the disease's severity. Unfortunately, the bacteria sometimes developed a resistance to the drug used to treat it. There were other drawbacks as well. Even patients for whom streptomycin worked often experienced unpleasant side effects.

The odds for recovering from TB improved when a second new drug used in combination with streptomycin was shown to enhance its potential. Finally, in 1952, TB became curable once a third drug was taken in conjunction with the first two.

The triumph of these drugs over a devastating disease changed the face of TB. Tuberculosis death rates plummeted, as what was once a national threat turned into a controllable illness. Sanitoriums across the country closed, as there were no longer any tuberculosis patients. Routine school screening programs for TB were suspended as well. Many thought that tuberculosis, like smallpox and cholera, had been conquered. But, regrettably, it resurfaced in 1985 in proportions threatening to rival its past.

3

BACK . . . NOT BY POPULAR DEMAND

Our national health care system is presently facing an old enemy. According to the National Institute of Allergy and Infectious Diseases of the National Institute of Health, TB has reemerged as a serious public health problem. In 1992 (the latest year for which statistics are available) a total of 26,673 active TB cases in all fifty states were reported to the Centers for Disease Control and Prevention. Besides people with active TB, an additional ten to fifteen million in the United States have latent (inactive) tuberculosis infections, which may someday develop into the disease.

So far, minority group members have been most affected by the recent TB outbreaks. In 1991, more than 56 percent of the active tuberculosis cases reported occurred among Hispanics and African Americans. In New York City, the disease has skyrocketed among black males, climbing to 345 active cases per 100,000 people.

Although TB can strike at any age, the largest increase has been among twenty-five- to forty-four-year-olds. In recent years, this group experienced a 52 percent rise in the disease. In addition, the incidence among children from birth to age four increased by 19 percent, while tuberculosis among five- to fourteen-year-olds rose by 40 percent.

Why did TB return? Physicians as well as social critics cite a number of reasons for the flare-up. But it's generally agreed that the war against tuberculosis stopped too soon. As late as 1969, the federal government was still channeling annually more than $20 million in TB project grants to local clinics and hospitals throughout the nation. But the declining TB rate made people feel that the crisis was over. So when the government began giving blocks of aid to states and municipalities to be used at the areas' discretion, the funding generally was not expended for TB control.

As time passed, countless successful TB programs were dismantled. In New York City alone, more than one thousand beds formerly reserved for TB patients were eliminated from municipal hospitals. Although outpatient services were supposed to be established to ensure the disease's continued decline, these were never made available. Instead, funding was diverted to meet more immediate needs. As one physician who's treated numerous TB victims described the situation, "We knew how to cure it. We had it in our hands. But we dropped the ball."[1]

Unfortunately, neither presidents Ronald Reagan nor George Bush made TB control a priority during their tenure in office. For the most part, TB research had been abandoned some years before, and there were few available avenues through which to restart it. According to Dr. Dixie E. Snyder, who for thirty years ran the TB program at the Centers for Disease Control and Prevention in Atlanta, "We had no real budget. We had to beg, borrow, and steal every dollar we could get. We had to get state and local hospitals to do studies for us because we had no funds. By the time we arrived in the eighties with a problem nobody could ignore, it was clear that we were in danger of losing the ability to handle this disease."[2]

The situation might have been somewhat alleviated in 1989, when the Department of Health and Human Services (HHS) backed an intricate TB control plan devised by the Centers for Disease Control and Prevention at an estimated annual cost of between $30 million and $34 million. The plan never took effect, however, because each year that it was proposed, the White House eliminated its funding from the budget.

The cost of a similar plan for 1993 would have been about $484 million, as a result of the disease's rapid spread. But the Clinton administration slashed the amount to $124 million, before sending the proposal to Congress. In commenting on the absence of government support for measures against TB, California representative Henry A. Waxman stated, "If there were such a thing as public health malpractice, all three administrations would be guilty."[3]

While the dearth of funding and programs for TB prevention set the stage for disaster, the growth of the AIDS epidemic worsened the predicament. A healthy individual's immune system serves to fend off illnesses. That's why people can harbor the TB bacterium in their bodies for years without ever experiencing the disease. However, if a person's immune system is compromised, as happens to someone with AIDS, a TB infection can quickly turn into an active case.

Therefore, when someone with AIDS is exposed to TB, he is at high risk of coming down with it. If his TB is not treated, the two infections can jointly shorten the individual's life. According to the United Nations World Health Organization, more than half of the AIDS patients exposed to tuberculosis will experience the disease in full force. A spokesperson for

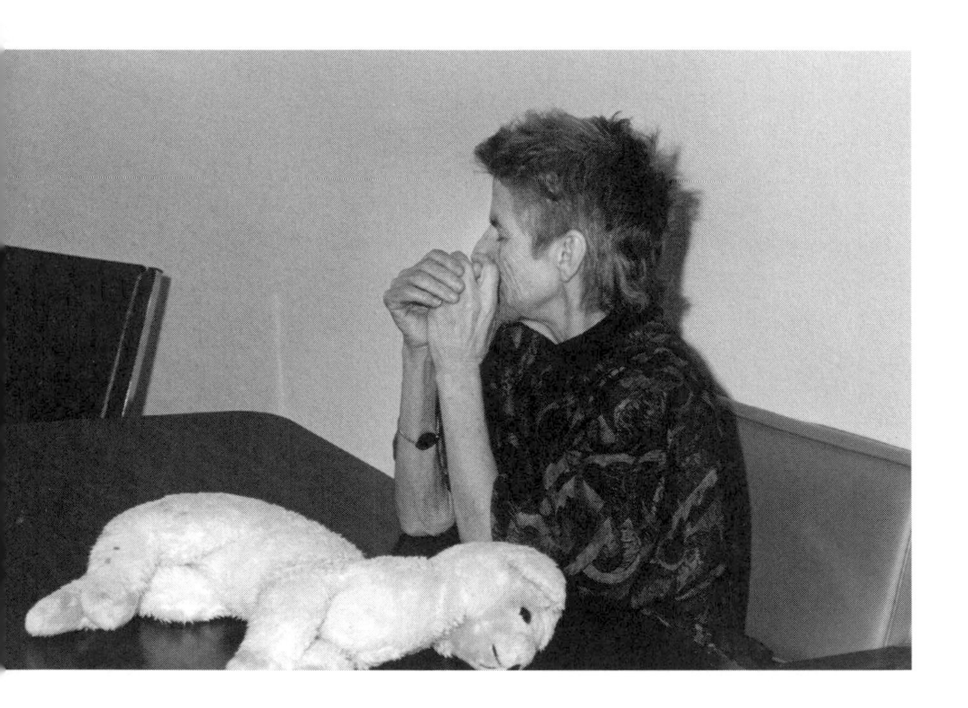

People with AIDS or other serious illnesses such as the woman shown here have compromised immune systems and are more vulnerable to TB.

the organization noted that AIDS may be the single "greatest risk factor" for active TB. This means that, as AIDS continues to spread, TB will as well. Perhaps Dr. Michael Iseman, of the National Jewish Center for Immunology and Respiratory Medicine, best summed up the growing problem, when he said, "If they don't die of something else first, virtually one hundred percent of the AIDS patients carrying TB bacteria will develop the illness."[4]

Another reason for TB's comeback is the lack of social welfare programs in 1980s. Severe government cuts in these areas left in dire straits significant numbers of Americans who were homeless, drug abusers, or infected with AIDS. Sick and destitute throngs of newly disenfranchised people were frequently packed into shelters or prisons. Many such places were poorly maintained, inadequately ventilated, and filled beyond their capacity. Often, the overcrowded and unsanitary living quarters resembled those of the working poor during the first TB epidemic. By largely disregarding the medical and housing needs of this growing population, a ripe environment for TB's return developed. As Dr. Michael Osterholm of the Minnesota Department of Public Health described the problem in 1992, "When we look back at the eighties, I think two social failures will stand out from all the others: the savings and loan crisis, and the return of TB."[5]

The situation is especially serious since under present conditions the disease is extremely difficult to contain. As TB is an airborne infection, the best way to limit widespread outbreaks is to isolate infected individuals while they are at the contagious stage. However, the places where TB is most rapidly spreading, such as homeless shelters or prisons, are often the least equipped to do so. In New York City, for example, nearly one-fifth of prison inmates have TB, but none of the jails have separately ventilated cells for contagious cases.

People living in homeless shelters and migrant farm workers, frequently selected from pools of homeless people, tend to fare as poorly. Usually, they are boarded in overcrowded rooms, shacks, or barracks that have inadequate or no ventilation. Generally, any time that a migrant worker takes off to seek medical attention is be subtracted from his wages.

In studying occupational accidents among these laborers, researchers at the University of North Carolina in Chapel Hill found that only one out of every three such injuries is ever medically treated. As a TB spe-

Widespread poverty has helped produce a ripe environment for TB's return.

cialist sarcastically commented on the likelihood of these individuals receiving ongoing treatment for TB, "If they can't get attention for a broken leg, they sure won't get it for a cough."[6] Yet tuberculosis is frequently spread through coughing.

In the early 1990s, federal funding to contend with rising TB rates was somewhat increased. Many felt, however, that the money came too late and was still insufficient. Once a disease such as tuberculosis escalates, curtailing it can be an extremely costly process. Furthermore, widespread TB control programs had been especially essential at this juncture because of the rise in drug-resistant strains of TB that do not respond to traditional antitubercular medication.

Drug-resistant TB initially occurs when TB patients do not take their prescribed medication for the specified time period. Generally, six to nine months of treatment with antitubercular drugs will cure most cases of TB. At times, however, some patients discontinue their medication within weeks because their symptoms have disappeared. If they become ill again, they continue to treat themselves only partially. This is actually worse than not taking any medication at all, because over a period of time the illness no longer responds to any form of medication, and they have, in fact, dissipated the drugs' effectiveness.

Unfortunately, significant numbers of people have misused their medication this way. The tendency to do so appears to cut across racial, class, and economic lines. "Of all TB patients, half do not take their medication as prescribed," cited Dr. Lee B. Reichman, president of the American Lung Association. "I'm not talking about poor inner-city dwellers or intravenous drug users, but doctors, reporters, and executives as well."[7]

As early as 1991, a Centers for Disease Control and Prevention study found that 14.1 percent of the new TB cases in the country did not respond to at least one drug while 3.3 percent of cases were resistant to two or more. The most recent reports from urban centers, however, indicate substantially higher rates. In New York City, one out of every three TB cases does not respond to at least one antitubercular drug and one out of every five is resistant to multiple drugs.

Prior to the late 1980s, doctors in the United States regarded drug-resistant tuberculosis as exceedingly rare and incapable of being transmitted from one person to another. But some early studies showed otherwise, and by the 1990s, lethal outbreaks of these virulent strains convinced the medical community that drug-resistant tuberculosis was indeed contagious.

Sadly, those with drug-resistant TB often readily transmit their disease to others who may later learn that they have few alternatives. This is a frightening trend, because untreated active TB kills more than two-thirds of its victims in two to three years, while multidrug-resistant strains (those that don't respond to a number of TB drugs used in combination) have fatality rates of at least 50 percent. "The public-health nightmare today is the emergence of an increasing number of drug-resistant strains," noted Dr. Charles Felton, chief of the pulmonary division of New York City's Harlem Hospital. His sentiments were underscored by a second physician, who said, "I haven't the foggiest notion what to do. There is no data. We are drug-bankrupt. Some patients are resistant to five, six, seven, eight drugs. . . . It's unbelievable."[8]

Physicians agree that treating drug-resistant strains of TB can be an arduous ordeal. Infected individuals may need to take drugs for years, which are as ravishing and debilitating to the system as chemotherapy. At times, patients may have to take between eighteen and twenty-four pills a day, while tolerating side effects that include nausea, drowsiness, hearing loss, dizziness, personality changes, and psychosis. In some cases, a portion of the patient's lung may need to be removed. Often, these individuals also have to contend with severe bouts of loneliness. Infected with a contagious disease that can be life-threatening, they frequently need to spend extensive periods of time isolated from others.

Some cases can even be worse as Tom Perkins (name changed), a thirty-five-year-old suffering from drug-resistant tuberculosis, found out. For an entire year he was quarantined at his mother's Tennessee home and

A lab technician works on identifying possible medications that might prove useful in combating various drug-resistant TB strains.

allowed to leave only for doctor's appointments. When his brothers and sisters visited his mother, they would wear protective masks to cover their mouth and nose. On those occasions, to make the others feel less uncomfortable, Tom usually waited outside the house, away from the rest of the family.

Yet apparently even that wasn't far enough away for everyone. Tom's friends abandoned him after learning about his illness, and a few of his siblings refused to come anywhere near the house. The only person Tom Perkins could count on seeing was the public health nurse who arrived each day to watch him swallow a combination of sixteen pills that his physician prescribed. But even that array of drugs failed to help him. The only discernible change in his condition was that after taking his medication he would be nauseous.

In addition to the pills, each week Tom had to endure three painful shots. When nothing seemed to work, his doctors resorted to surgically draining fluid from his lungs. Yet after a year of intensive treatment, the still very ill patient evaluated his condition this way: "I was losing ground. I was losing weight. I was short of breath. I was tired all the time. I was really depressed and lonely."[9]

In a final attempt to save his life, Tom Perkins's physicians sent him to the National Jewish Center for Immunology and Respiratory Medicine in Denver, Colorado, which specializes in treating drug-resistant TB. There he could benefit from the most advanced and aggressive, if unpleasant, therapies available in the world. In Perkins's case, this entailed a grueling operation to remove his entire right lung as well as the lining of his chest wall. The chief physician of the TB service described the facility's philosophy as follows: "We are willing to gamble on very painful and risky treatments, because this is their [the patients'] last shot. If we can't control their disease, they die the death of consumption, slowly strangled as TB eats away at their lungs."[10]

Besides the human costs involved, drug-resistant tuberculosis is also considerably more expensive to treat. The Centers for Disease Control and Prevention estimate that the entire medical bill for a standard TB case, including medication, supervised therapy, and medical examinations, is approximately $11,000. On the other hand, the amount needed to care for a patient with a TB strain resistant to two or more drugs is upward of $250,000.

Each case of drug-resistant TB is a tragedy for both the affected individual and society at large. If the problem isn't curbed quickly, America could soon find itself faced with a rapidly spreading epidemic and no effective means to fight it.

4

QUESTIONS AND ANSWERS ABOUT TB

The recent spread of TB in the United States makes it necessary for everyone to know as much as possible about the disease, as well as discarding any misinformation or irrational fears about it. This question-and-answer chapter seeks to separate myth from reality, while arming you with what you need to know to help you stay well.

Question: What is tuberculosis (TB)?
Answer: Tuberculosis, called TB for short, is an infectious disease caused by the microorganism *Mycobacterium tuberculosis*. Although TB can strike anywhere in the body (such as the brain, kidney, or spine), it usually affects the lungs. No one is born with TB—the disease must be acquired. It is transmitted by repeated exposure to airborne droplets that have been contaminated with *Mycobacterium tuberculosis*. These germs may be sprayed into the air if a person with active TB of the lungs or throat coughs, sneezes, laughs, or sings.

Question: What are the symptoms of TB?
Answer: TB's most common symptoms include feeling weak or ill, loss of appetite, weight loss without dieting, fever, and/or night sweats. These signs may last for several weeks or more and usually worsen if the person doesn't receive treatment. With TB of the lungs, the individual may cough incessantly, bringing up mucus, phlegm, or blood. The person may also experience chest pain when coughing. TB sometimes mimics other ailments, and in various instances has initially been mistaken for a cold, the flu, or severe bronchitis. Unfortunately, physicians who aren't familiar with TB in areas where it's still relatively rare may not even consider it when diagnosing a patient.

Question: Who gets TB?
Answer: Anyone, regardless of age, race, sex, or financial status, can get TB. However, some people are at a higher risk of contracting the disease than others. The Centers for Disease Control and Prevention's Division of Tuberculosis Elimination cites the following groups as belonging to that category:

- Poor people
- Homeless people
- Foreign-born people from countries where TB is widespread
- Nursing-home residents
- Prisoners in correctional facilities
- People with medical conditions such as diabetes, certain types of cancer, or being underweight
- People with AIDS
- Persons receiving immunosuppresive therapy

Question: What's the difference between a TB infection and the TB disease itself?

A group of men gather outside a homeless shelter in Sacramento, California. The Centers for Disease Control and Prevention's Division of Tuberculosis Elimination cites homeless people as among those at high risk.

Answer: TB occurs in two stages. The first is known as inactive TB or TB infection, in which the germ that causes tuberculosis lies dormant in the body. As the person's immune system maintains a standoff with the infection, individuals with inactive TB do not transmit the illness to others. Those with TB infection have a 5 percent chance of developing active TB throughout their lifetime. The risk is highest during the first year of infection, but in some cases TB disease does not occur until many years later. Active TB is more likely to develop in these individuals if their immune system is weakened during treatment for kidney transplantation, or as a result of diabetes, cancer, malnutrition, or AIDS. Medication is frequently prescribed for individuals with inactive TB infection to prevent them from developing active TB.

In active TB, or TB disease, the microorganism responsible for the illness has begun to multiply and spread to various organs of the body, causing destruction. Although the pulmonary form (TB of the lungs) is best known, examples of other forms of the disease are not rare. In literature, the hunchback of Notre Dame had TB of the vertebrae (Pott's Disease), while former First Lady Eleanor Roosevelt died of undiagnosed tuberculosis of the bone marrow. TB of the brain and spinal cord, known as TB meningitis, and scrofula, or TB of the lymph nodes, are still other forms. Anyone with TB disease must secure medical attention—those who do not significantly lower their chances of survival.

Question: How can you tell if you have TB infection?
Answer: A tuberculin test, sometimes called the Mantoux test or skin test, is the only way to know if someone has TB infection. In most cases, the test is done on the person's arm. A small needle is used to place the testing material, known as tuberculin, beneath the skin. In two to three days, the area is checked to see if there was a reaction to the test. A bump about the size of a pencil eraser or larger will appear on the person's arm if the test is "positive"—indicating that the individual has TB infection. Someone who has had prolonged exposure to TB, but nevertheless has a negative skin test, may wish to be retested a few weeks later, just to be certain the result was correct.

Though skin tests for TB are commonly used, they may not always be reliable for people with AIDS or other illnesses that result in a breakdown of the immune system. These individuals will need other tests to determine if they're infected. People who are tested too soon after exposure may have a false negative reaction as well. It generally takes between two to ten weeks following exposure for the skin test to yield a positive reaction.

Question: How can you tell if you have TB disease?
Answer: While the tuberculin test (see above) shows that TB germs are present in a person's body, a positive reaction does not necessarily mean that the person has TB disease. To identify TB disease, doctors must have additional tests performed. These include the following:

- The Chest X Ray: If a person has TB disease that's affected his lungs, the subsequent deterioration will appear as a shadow on a chest X ray. In these instances, some physicians have their patients' X rays repeated over a period of time to note any changes in the shadow that might indicate the disease's progression.
- The Sputum Test: In this procedure, a sample of the patient's coughed-up sputum is examined under a microscope for evidence of the microorganism responsible for tuberculosis. Some physicians have three separate samples taken to ensure accuracy.

In addition to these tests, thorough physical examinations assist physicians in diagnosing TB disease.

Question: Can you catch TB from sitting at a bus stop next to someone who has it?
Answer: Extremely unlikely. As the majority of people with TB expel relatively few bacilli or germs, the disease is usually only transmitted after prolonged

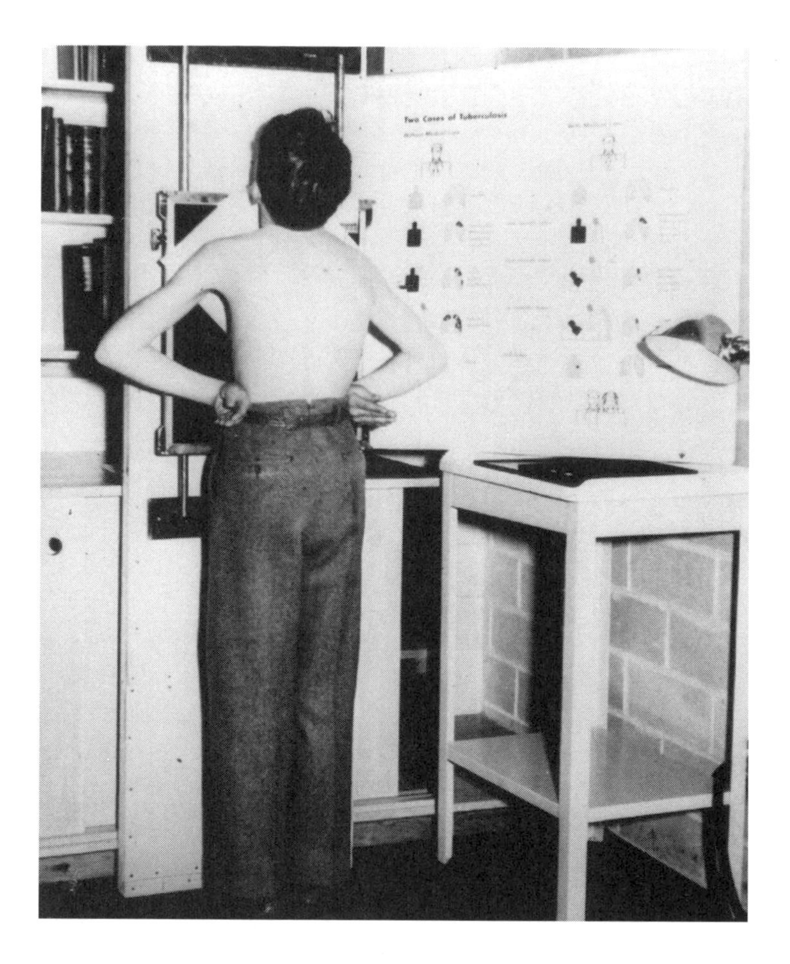

Chest X rays as shown here have been used through the years as a TB detection tool.

exposure to someone with TB disease. Researchers estimate that, on the average, people have a 50 percent chance of becoming infected if they spend the following amounts of time either living or working with someone who has active tuberculosis:

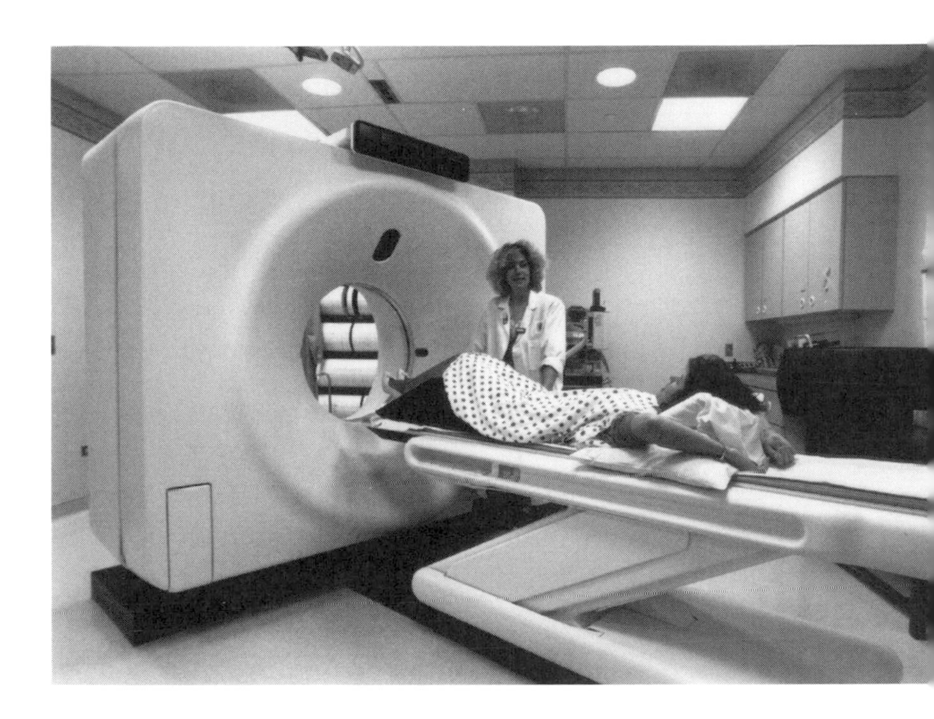

This CT scanner, specifically built to provide images of the lungs, has been extremely helpful in diagnosing TB cases.

- Eight hours a day for six months
- Twenty-four hours a day for two months

As TB is basically an airborne disease, it's unlikely to be transmitted through personal items such as clothing, bedding, books or other things that a person with TB disease might have touched.

Question: Is TB curable?
Answer: Most cases of TB can be cured if diagnosed early and effective treatment is instituted without delay. This is achieved through taking antituberculosis

drugs, as prescribed. Patients should not alter the amount of medication or the length of time indicated. If someone stops his medication too soon, he can develop a drug-resistant strain of the disease, which is considerably harder to cure.

Question: What is multidrug-resistant tuberculosis (MDR-TB) and who can get it?
Answer: Multidrug-resistant tuberculosis is a TB strain that does not respond to the available medications used to fight TB. The U.S. Department of Health and Human Services cites the following groups as at high risk for MDR-TB:

- Persons who have recently been exposed to MDR-TB especially if they are immuno-compromised (have a weakened immune system)
- TB patients who fail to take their medication as prescribed
- Patients who were put on an ineffective treatment regime
- Persons previously treated for TB

Although multidrug-resistant TB is spreading, it is currently most prevalent in New York City, Miami, Florida, and Newark, New Jersey.

Question: Will we ever be able to control TB?
Answer: Numerous health care and social changes must be instituted to stem the growing tide of tuberculosis. The following measures, however, would be an important start:

- Antituberculosis drug treatment should be initiated for persons with TB disease, to render them noninfectious.

- Persons at high risk for TB infection should be screened and, if infected, evaluated for protective therapy.
- Ongoing TB screening should be provided to health care workers who have regular contact with persons with TB or AIDS (a particularly high-risk condition for TB).

Question: Have more young people been affected by the recent rise in TB?
Answer: Yes. The Centers for Disease Control and Prevention report that tuberculosis among young people fifteen and under has risen 35 percent since 1985. According to Dr. Ida Onorato, the center's chief of tuberculosis surveillance, "They're the second wave of TB. Their parents . . . either don't know they have TB until they've already exposed their families, or they don't get proper treatment."

Although the number of infected children remains small, compared to that of adults, health officials are concerned because they see few ways to protect these youths. As Dr. Onorato continues, "Until we can reach all persons who need to be screened, get them on medication . . . there's going to continue to be transmission to children."[1]

5

THE INTERNATIONAL SCENE

Zheng Xumin, a sixty-seven-year-old retired college professor from Beijing, China, took an extended beach vacation, hoping to clear up the severe cough that had been troubling him. When he failed to improve, however, he sought medical attention and learned that he had an active case of TB. After successfully completing an intensive six-month treatment, Zheng Xumin was pronounced cured. It is impossible, however, to say how many people he infected during his stay at the shore.

Zheng Xumin was among the fortunate ones. Annually, about a quarter of a million people in China die as a result of tuberculosis. Most of the victims are peasants, and throughout the Chinese countryside there's a saying that goes, "Ten get it, nine die."

Unfortunately, tuberculosis remains a problem of vast international proportions. Every year, it kills more people worldwide than any other infection, including malaria and AIDS. Presently, at least a third of the world's population is infected with TB, which puts them at risk for developing TB disease. It is also estimated that approximately thirty million people will die from tuberculosis during the next ten years. Although TB has recently resurfaced in industrialized nations, about 95 percent of the eight million annual cases occur in developing regions of Asia, Africa, and Latin America.

Poverty, malnutrition, and inadequate sanitation make various populations especially vulnerable to tuberculosis. As in the United States, the spread of AIDS has significantly worsened the situation as well. The Caribbean and sub-Saharan Africa are among the worst-hit areas. In some African cities, nearly 80 percent of the TB patients also have AIDS—three times as many as five years ago. Researchers feel that, without intervention, the number of cases could rise even twelve times as high.

Once effective drugs against TB were developed, it was assumed that Third World countries would use them to control the illness. But things didn't turn out that way. The TB drugs proved not to be as readily available as initially assumed. While these medications were relatively inexpensive, compared to some others, even their minimal cost was taxing for the limited economic resources of many developing nations.

In addition, organizing effective far-reaching programs was especially challenging in numerous countries. Political instability and ongoing internal strife in some areas made establishing interconnecting health services difficult, if not impossible. At times even the most commonly used TB diagnostic tests could not be easily adapted to the rural areas of poorer nations, as well-maintained, on-site equipment and trained lab technicians were generally necessary.

The United Nations' World Health Organization (WHO) has taken a vital role in fighting the worldwide TB epidemic. The organization's Tuberculosis Programme actively promoted the development of en-

Frequently slum areas in poor nations, such as this one in India, face widespread TB outbreaks.

hanced tools to diagnose, treat, and prevent the disease. Because of the dearth of available resources for tuberculosis research, WHO attempts to ensure that global efforts in this arena be properly coordinated, to avoid unnecessary duplication and waste. At times, this may entail encouraging communication and joint projects among the various groups involved in TB research, as well as reaching out for ideas and resources to specialists in other fields.

Educational forums have frequently facilitated this goal. In April 1993, the London School of Hygiene and Tropical Medicine sponsored a public health seminar called "Tuberculosis—Back to the Future." The gathering drew immunologists, epidemiologists, economists, clinicians, health administrators, and heads of TB control programs from fifty-six countries. Other WHO objectives include having the public health community alert politicians internationally to the danger posed by the increase of tuberculosis cases. Elected officials must be reminded of the connection between poverty and TB, and the importance of funneling resources to the poorer areas of the world where TB is most prevalent.

Some important inroads have already been made in a number of developing nations. As early as 1977, the United Republic of Tanzania established a well-received National Tuberculosis and Leprosy Program (NTLP). Its success is at least partly the result of the government's commitment to the project's work. It's a broad-based effort run by a nearly all-Tanzanian staff whose salaries and benefits are government-funded. Yet the program could not have survived without international assistance. The medication needed for treatment is supplied by overseas donors, as is the money for training and staff supervision. In addition, the cars and motorbikes enabling health workers to reach patients in more distant parts of the country are donated from outside sources.

The program's basic goals are as follows:

- To find all TB cases
- To treat all cases until cured and thus eliminate a source of infection to others
- To monitor the results achieved in each district, to maintain high rates of cure[1]

It's estimated that, as a result of the project, 80 percent of Tanzanian TB victims were identified and 90 percent of these individuals received treatment. NTLP's cure rate is presently about 80 percent. Although Tanzania's efforts are exemplary, the problem is still far from solved. Unfortunately, despite their diligent work, the number of TB cases in Tanzania has increased because of the spread of AIDS.

Additional examples of innovative intervention in the fight against TB has been evident in a number of other developing countries. As was mentioned earlier, tuberculosis is extremely prevalent in rural regions of China, where annual death rates climb to as high as a quarter of a million people. Although the country had a tuberculosis control program, it had not been effective because of insufficient funding. In the early 1990s, however, a sizable loan was obtained through the World Bank to revitalize the project in twelve provinces, which would ultimately benefit 550 million people.

The plan was aimed at improving case detection and enhancing treatment. Village health workers were recruited and trained in various aspects of identifying and curing infectious patients. Through this endeavor, in 1992, more than 20,000 new as well as formerly treated TB victims received the help they needed. International health agencies hope that China's success will demonstrate how significant gains against TB can be made, even in deprived rural areas where previous TB control programs have failed.

Although tuberculosis is especially prevalent in many underdeveloped parts of the world, the scope of the problem is significantly broader. In recent years, TB rates have also risen in industrialized countries besides the United States. Western Europe has been affected by this growing global epidemic, as Denmark, Ireland, Italy, the Netherlands, Norway, Spain, and Switzerland have all reported an increased number of tuberculosis cases. Tuberculosis also exists in Australia, Sweden, and the United Kingdom, but the number of the new cases in these countries appears to have leveled off. The elderly population has been largely affected in Western Europe, although AIDS is also an undeniable factor in contributing to increased TB rates in parts of France as well as Italy, Spain, and Portugal.

WHO partly attributes the resurgence of TB in industrialized nations to a combination of public complacency and the ease in international travel. A study by the agency indicated that "twenty-seven percent of all new cases in the United States last year [1992] were in victims who had recently come from another country."[2] With improved transportation making distant parts of the world more accessible, the same phenomenon is occurring around the globe. WHO further noted that "an increase in TB funding, [along with a] change in direction, is the only way to avert a health catastrophe."[3] Numerous medical experts believe that the combined talents and resources of academic institutions, the pharmaceutical industry, international organizations, and the world political community are necessary to tackle and defeat the rising tide of tuberculosis.

Each year, approximately eight million new cases of tuberculosis and three million TB-related deaths occur. The disease is responsible for 18.5 percent of all deaths among people between fifteen and fifty-nine years of age, as well as 26 percent of avoidable deaths. Ideally, a practical multidisciplinary TB control plan might be devised through an exchange of ideas and open discussion. The United Nations' TB Programme has provided a valuable start by already working with governments throughout the world to develop effective tracking and monitoring procedures.

Many feel it's up to the industrial nationals to provide the impetus for a global program before the crisis and costs escalate out of hand. These measures are crucial, as it's become increasingly clear that if tuberculosis isn't effectively curtailed in developing nations, it will remain uncontrolled throughout the world.

6

PROGNOSIS FOR THE FUTURE

Since the early 1990s, U.S. medical professionals and health care advocates have actively stressed the impending danger of the rapidly growing TB epidemic. Yet, because they think of tuberculosis as a disease that primarily affects the homeless, prison inmates, and AIDS victims, many Americans remain unconcerned, believing they are safe. Actually, nothing could be further from the truth. As an airborne disease, tuberculosis can be readily spread, and it is already beginning to turn up in areas where it was never expected to surface.

That's what happened to the Hallie family, who reside in North Tarrytown, an affluent Westchester County suburb of New York City. Their neighborhood, characterized by beautifully furnished homes and lovely landscapes, bore no relationship to the squalid homeless shelters that had become known breeding grounds for TB. Yet in January 1992, four months after the Hallies' twins were born, TB impacted on their lives.

The parents noticed that one of the infants had developed a cold and wheezing cough that lingered on. Although doctors couldn't initially pinpoint the problem, they eventually determined that the child had tuberculosis. When the baby's family was tested, it was further found that the infant's twin as well as the father had active TB (TB disease), while the mother and older brother (age five) were both infected.

The family was taken aback by the news. "I felt so immune," remarked the twins' mother, Michelena Hallie, a New York attorney. "We live in a tiny town in Westchester, in the middle of the forest. My kids never come into the city. We were totally floored."[1] The Hallies still don't know how they contracted TB. But out of forty of their friends, relatives, and coworkers who were subsequently tested for the disease, four were also found to be infected.

The Hallies' experience is not an isolated episode. Health authorities report that tuberculosis cases are increasingly cropping up in suburban and farm regions, far from the urban centers where the disease's resurgence originally began. Unfortunately, health care practitioners in these areas are often largely unfamiliar with TB and have little awareness of the disease. This may result in insufficient TB screening and reluctance to diagnose it.

Many suburban and rural hospitals also aren't outfitted with the necessary laboratory equipment to yield a speedy diagnosis. And if a patient lives anywhere from two to four hours from the nearest medical facility, follow-up becomes more difficult. Even once a TB case has been identified, treatment may not be adequately aggressive if tuberculosis is not perceived as a significant health threat to the community.

Although the incidence of tuberculosis in outlying areas is still relatively low, it's essential to act before the numbers grow. The setting is ripe for an epidemic, because parts of rural America are now experiencing problems, such as poverty, drug abuse, AIDS, and immigration from countries with high TB rates, that significantly contributed to major outbreaks in cities. A large number of TB cases outside urban areas have also resulted from old infections that were activated through aging, malnutrition, or immune system impairment. As Mrs. Hallie summed up her feelings about her family's experience with TB, "Nobody's safe, if we aren't."[2]

Many people in Bath, Maine, would agree. TB was almost unknown in the small town of 10,000, until 1989 when one man gave the disease to more than 400 people. Upon investigation, health authorities found that neither poverty nor AIDS was a factor in this instance. Apparently, a man working as a metal grinder at a Bath shipyard simply didn't know that he had active TB. He had seen a doctor who failed to recognize the illness, and as a result had spread the disease for more than eight months until he had been properly diagnosed.

Of the numerous shipyard workers eventually tested by health authorities, 417 were found to be infected. Physicians speculate that the dust, as well as the cramped working conditions, aboard the vessels provided an ideal environment for the disease's spread. The patient's coworkers, however, weren't the only ones affected. Three of the thirty patrons at a tavern that the man often frequented were infected as well. In the end, twenty-five of the thirty people that he either closely worked or socialized with tested positive for TB.

Health officials stress that the disease's rampant spread in Maine should serve as a warning to areas that may not perceive TB as a real threat. As Dr. Ban Mishu of Vanderbilt University, who investigated the Bath incident, noted, "This population was not typical of the new outbreak of the 1980s and 1990s. This demonstrates the need for proper control of TB, even in low-risk populations."[3]

Other parts of the country have already been unexpectedly stricken as well. In 1992, an Arkansas woman working in a chicken-processing plant on the Oklahoma border, infected scores of people. Out of about 150 individuals tested for TB, approximately 100 required treatment. When the woman became too fatigued to continue at her job at the plant, she began caring for neighborhood children—placing them at risk as well. The disease has taken even greater toll in countless locales. For instance, in the sixteen counties surrounding Houston, Texas, new TB cases rose by 80 percent between 1989 and 1992.

The danger to the population is even more acutely felt by those who work with tuberculosis victims. Having adjusted to the somewhat minuscule danger of contracting AIDS on the job, health care professionals now find that tuberculosis has become a far more serious threat—particularly since increased cases of drug-resistant strains make the risk even more lethal. In discussing the problem, the chief medical resident at a Newark, New Jersey, hospital said, "The first thing in my mind is that I'm breathing the same air. I'm pretty concerned about getting infected. I really don't want to bring it home to my kids."[4]

Numerous health care workers have declined positions that would entail frequent close contact with TB patients, while others are planning to leave the profession altogether.[5] For some, it may already be too late. A case in point is that of Dr. Beth Malasky, who became infected with what might prove a drug-resistant strain of TB during her last year of medical school. As she summed up her predicament, "When I started in medicine, the prospect of being exposed to TB was not a big deal since there were drugs to treat it, but now it's a life-threatening disease."[6] Malasky completed a prescribed course of four drugs, but she can't

A clinic nurse calls in a patient to be seen. Health care workers often find themselves at high risk for TB.

be sure she's cured, because there are still no guarantees in treating drug-resistant TB. The young physician feels her illness will influence her future medical practice plans.

Unfortunately, what happened to Dr. Malasky is becoming increasingly common among physicians, nurses, and various other health care workers who come in frequent contact with large numbers of TB patients. In the early 1990s, a survey at Chicago's Cook County Hospital revealed that 46 percent of the medical interns were already infected with tuberculosis, while in New York City the rate was between 10 and 30 percent among a comparable group.

By 1993, the Dallas County medical examiner, along with eight of twenty-one staff members working in the autopsy room, tested positive for tuberculosis. Unfortunately, they had inhaled the bacteria as the chests of TB victims had been sawed open during autopsies. Those working with tuberculosis patients in other capacities are also frequently adversely affected. Twenty-three percent of prison inmates in New York State are infected with TB, as are 6 percent of the staff as well.

Undeniable evidence of the growing TB epidemic has fueled the present call for change. But although it's acknowledged that something must be done, not everyone agrees on what. The debate continues as to what is the most cost-effective way to control TB as well as what's possible in the immediate future. Meanwhile the measures below are among those most frequently discussed:

Improved Testing Measures: New diagnostic tools feasible for international use are sorely needed. Dr. Charles Peloquin, director of the pharmacokinetics laboratory at the National Jewish Center for Immu-

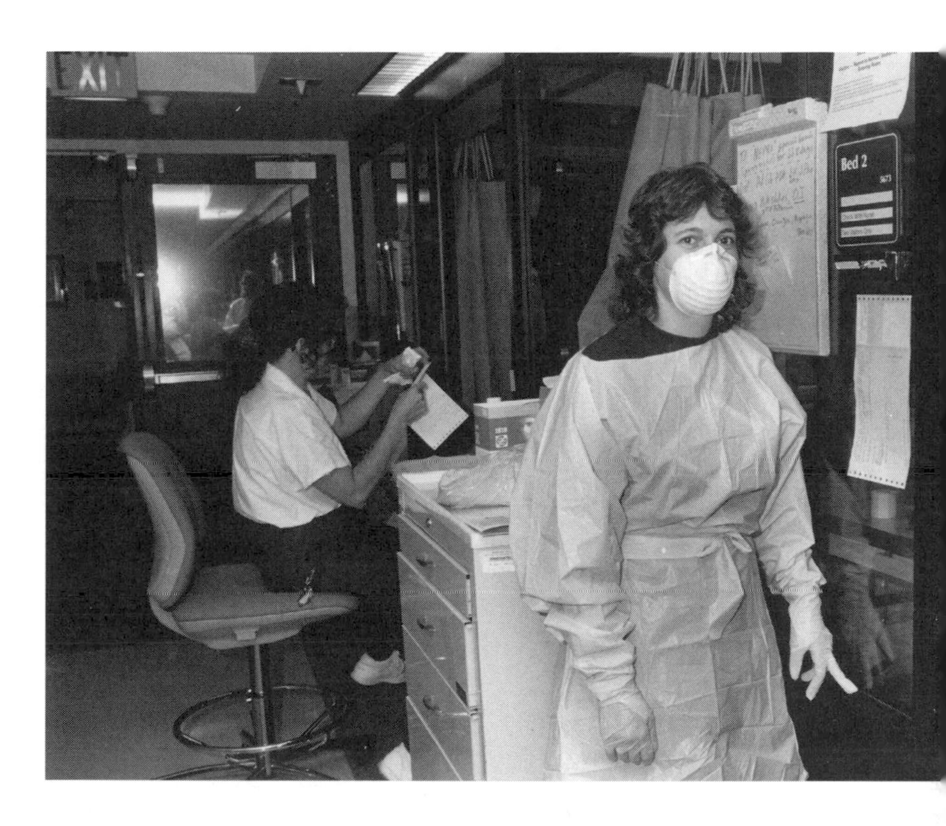

A nurse at a hospital isolation ward wears protective garb when working with contagious patients.

nology, has pointed out that since the microorganism responsible for tuberculosis is extremely slow growing, it can take between eight to twelve weeks to develop in the sputum culture that is used for testing for active TB. Such diagnostic delays frequently lead to lengthy delays in treating this highly infectious killer. Recently, some hospitals and commercial testing companies have begun using newly developed radiometric and genetic testing methods to check more speedily for TB microorganisms. These permit labs to secure results in a day or two rather than waiting for weeks, but as of yet their use is not widespread.

Improved Medications to Fight TB: Bacille Calmette Guerin (BCG), a TB vaccine developed in the early 1920s, is still widely used by the World Health Organization in developing countries to protect children and young adults from tuberculosis. The vaccine, however, is far from perfect, as various batches frequently vary greatly. Many U.S. physicians view BCG as a somewhat flawed TB control measure. Although American health care professionals acknowledge that BCG may reduce the risk of the disease by as much as 50 percent in youths, its value for adults is dubious. Still another negative feature of the vaccine is that it renders the standard skin test for TB infection useless. Anyone who has been vaccinated will test positive regardless of whether or not he's actually infected.

Experts stress that more research is necessary to develop new vaccines. Scientists may have to call on the available modern tools of molecular biology, immunology, and genetics for an answer. Genetic engineering may eventually enable them to manipulate the TB organism to immunize people effectively with minimal risk.

Besides a vaccine, new drugs for treatment are necessary as well. Researchers hope to screen presently available drugs to see if any might be useful in combating tuberculosis. Ironically, the medication isoniazid, an effective antitubercular drug, was around for forty years before its benefits were fully realized. In working on still another approach, the National Institute of Allergy and Infectious Disease is exploring the possibility of developing an implantable drug for patients who are unreliable about taking their medication.

This photograph, taken some years ago, shows a line of six-year-olds waiting for their TB vaccinations.

Improved Facilities: Fighting an airborne disease involves instituting important structural changes in various facilities where tuberculosis is likely to be transmitted. Ideally, hospitalized TB patients should be in "negative-pressure" rooms, where air flows directly from a central area to their quarters before being vented outside. With this system, fresh air is pumped to the patient six times an hour, while the air he breathes is not recirculated. Negative-pressure airflow would significantly reduce the number of airborne germs escaping into the halls, where others might be exposed to them. Until such changes are instituted, exhaust fans may be installed in the TB patients' rooms to draw contaminated air out.

Many facilities, such as hospitals, drug treatment centers, and homeless shelters, are also installing ultraviolet lights to kill TB germs in the air. In addition, those who work with tuberculosis victims must either learn or relearn what precautions to take against airborne diseases. This may include wearing gloves, gowns, and surgical masks, when appropriate, although for extra protection some health care employees prefer wearing hoodlike, industrial respirator masks. Patients with tuberculosis should also use close-fitting masks when taken from their rooms to various areas of the hospital for testing or other necessary medical procedures. At all other times, they should remain in their rooms, behind closed doors, with signs stating Infection Control Precautions.

While reducing the spread of the microorganisms responsible for TB would undoubtedly help control the disease, in many areas these measures have not been rapidly instituted. Often, the delay has been the result of a lack of agreement on the necessary standards, coupled with a dearth of financial resources for planning and implementation. The physical restructuring of hospitals, shelters, and prisons presents a monumental expense at a time when funding in these areas is already stretched to the limit.

As a result, numerous institutions across America have failed to adequately protect their employees and in some situations even questioned the claims of staff members that they contracted the disease through their jobs. Darryl D. James developed active TB while employed as a maintenance worker at a New York

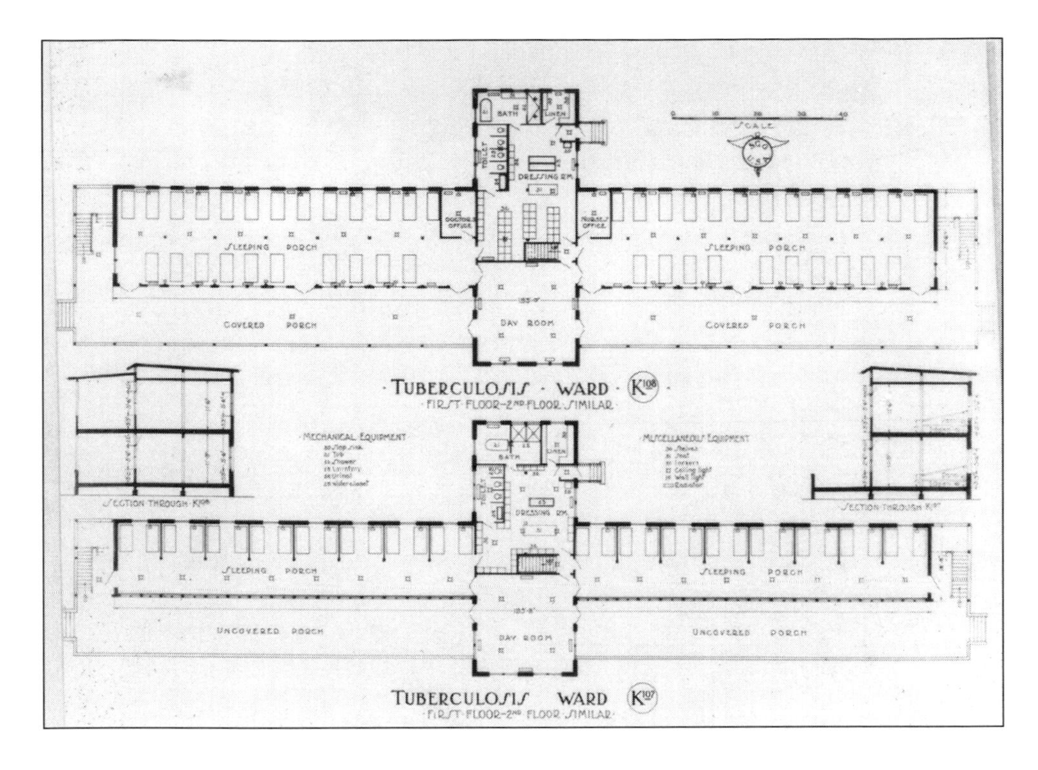

A diagram of an early hospital tuberculosis ward. Today, numerous institutions are being structurally redesigned to help contain the disease.

City hospital. James became extremely ill, losing thirty pounds in one month and afterward missing fourteen months of work. Yet despite his suffering, his employer refused to acknowledge the source of his problem. Instead, management doctors responded to his predicament by simply asking, "How do you know you got it here; maybe you got it on the train or bus?"[7] James was strongly discouraged from seeking worker's compensation benefits and ended up on welfare while applying for back pay.

In another instance, an occupational therapist who became infected with TB while working at a hospital decided to look for a different job. The change was motivated more by her employer's indifference to what had happened than by her concern about TB. She said, "It makes me not want to work in hospitals."[8]

When officials from the Centers for Disease Control and Prevention investigated an outbreak of drug-resistant TB among patients and health care workers at one of the hospitals, they found that the workers' complaints regarding their employer's lax attitude were justified. At the time, patients with infectious cases of TB were found watching TV in lounges and walking down the facility's corridors without masks.

The medical unit chief, who recognized a similar situation at one of New York City's detention centers, noted, "You didn't have to be a rocket scientist to realize there were pneumonias here that weren't getting any better. We knew our screening program was problematic and that TB was being spread here. . . ."[9] Nevertheless, crucial warnings that might have curtailed the epidemic's spread through the state's penal institutions went unheeded. To the horror of employees, the media later revealed that for more than two and half years state officials had ignored a health department warning about a TB outbreak among AIDS-infected inmates.

Unfortunately, in some cases even well-intentioned plans to install useful measures have gone awry, resulting in a loss of valuable time and resources. A prime example of this is what happened at Riker's Island, a short-term detention center in New York City. Disastrous renovations included the installation of unusable ultraviolet lights, which were so bright that they caused eye strain, and noisy aluminum ventilation ducts that kept inmates up all night. The prison finally had to abandon its work and start from scratch.

After careful planning, a scheme was adopted for Riker's Island that included constructing isolation cells for contagious prisoners, at a cost of $450,000 each. There was also a computer-based inmate tracking system to prevent those with active TB from being lost in the state's extensive penal network. TB-detection methods were improved as well by obtaining chest X rays for all new prisoners. The prison's efforts now stand as a model for other facilities grappling with this problem.

In addition to structural and financial obstacles, there are frequently attitudinal differences as to how TB sufferers should be handled. A number of health care professionals simply aren't comfortable wearing protective garb that could psychologically separate them from their patient. As one physician who felt that way stated, "We have to build relationships with such patients, and if doctors have to get into space suits and wear gas masks, patients aren't going to take their pills. It's probably much more important to teach TB patients to cover their mouths when they cough."[10]

Some medical experts believe the answer to controlling tuberculosis lies in isolating infectious patients as well as ensuring that they take their medication as prescribed. Although many contagious TB patients are willing to remain largely isolated in their homes while they're being treated, this isn't true for everyone. As a result, health care authorities are left to ponder the question: How do you protect society from those with highly infectious diseases without infringing on these individuals' rights?

In December 1992, thirty-four scientists, ethicists, and public health officials formed a voluntary panel to evaluate the predicament and map out possible solutions. They issued a report titled "The Tuberculosis Revival," which contained a number of controversial and far-reaching solutions to curtail the epidemic.

Among these was a proposal for the passage of new legislation requiring that TB patients be observed directly when taking their medication. These regulations would apply to all TB victims, regardless of social class or financial status. "It is absolutely essential that we never again draw lines in health care between the haves and the have-nots," noted one of the panel members.[11]

But will stopping TB's spread ultimately entail detaining large numbers of people for treatment against their will? The Lemuel Shattuck Hospital outside Boston, Massachusetts, set up a small ward for TB patients who will not take their medication voluntarily. The ward is locked—patients sent there by a judge are not permitted to leave before being medically discharged. Some patients must be brought forcefully to such facilities, and at least one individual arrived at Lemuel Shattuck Hospital handcuffed.

Many cities, however, do not have special centers or hospital wards for TB patients. Instead, they are placed in hospital rooms that would normally be used by someone with a highly infectious disease who had voluntarily entered the hospital. The treatment is the same, only in these cases an armed guard is posted outside the room twenty-four hours a day, at a weekly cost of nearly two thousand dollars. Besides the crippling expense of caring for these individuals, most hospitals do not like to treat chronically uncooperative tuberculosis patients because 73 percent of them have drug-resistant TB, which poses special risks to the staff.

Presently, more than forty states have laws permitting public health officials to detain TB patients as long as they're infectious. The bulk of this legislation was passed at the turn of the century, when TB posed a lethal threat to America. So far, the number of patients forcefully detained remains relatively small. In New York City, thirty-three such detention orders

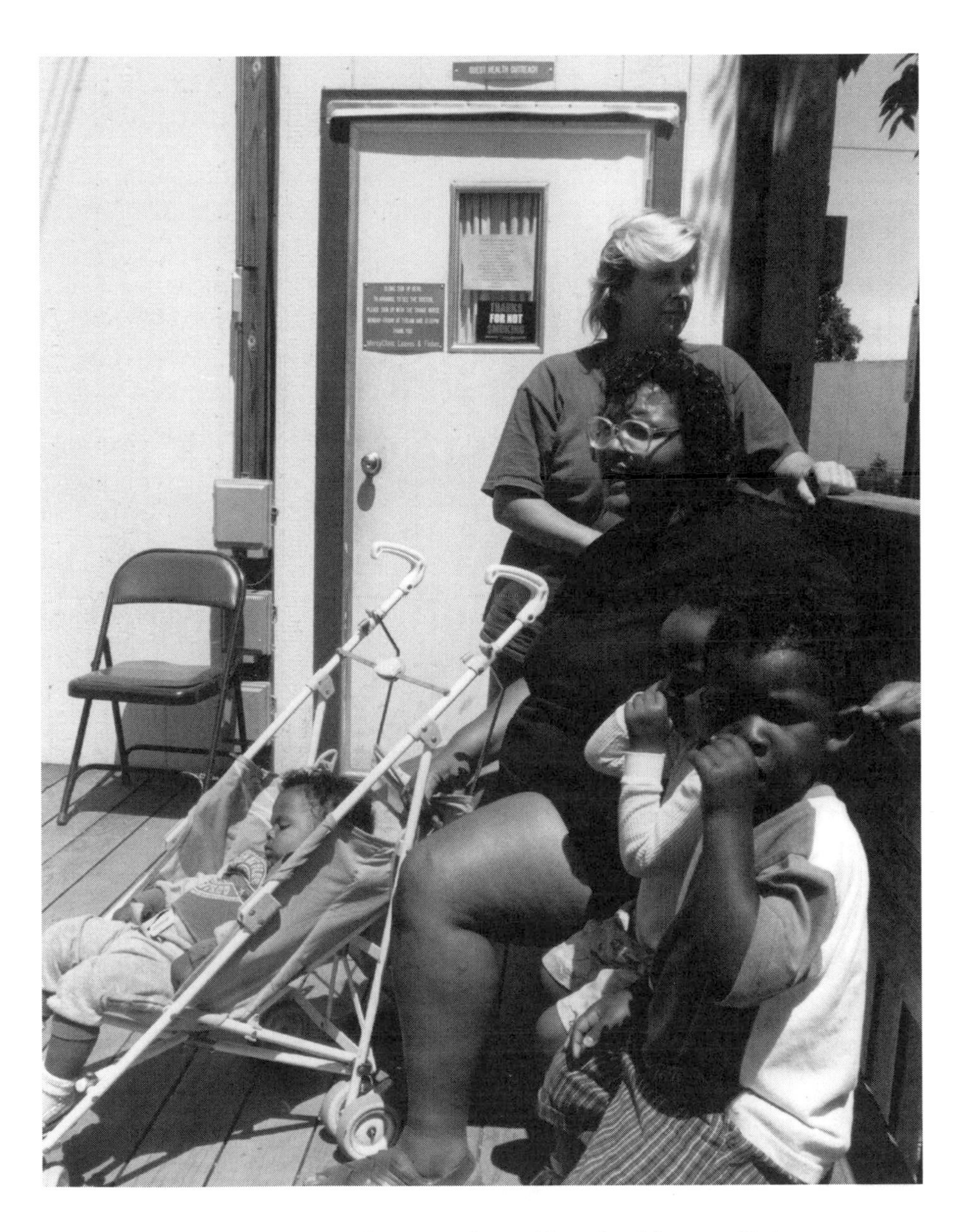

Patients wait to be treated outside a health care clinic. Access to adequate medical treatment is crucial in preventing the spread of TB and other contagious diseases.

were issued between 1988 and 1990, and another forty-four in 1991.

Yet some people feel that even these are too many. Critics of detaining recalcitrant TB patients argue that the practice is discriminatory. They stress that it's usually minority-group members, the poor, homeless, or mentally ill who are locked away—people who have never had access to decent health care to begin with. They believe that having TB and attempting to get well is difficult enough without incurring the threat of imprisonment as well. As one impoverished TB victim described what trying to recover was like for him, "They make it sound so easy. I have to take four kinds of pills three times a day. They make me sick. Sometimes I have to come here [to the treatment clinic] and sit and wait for my pills. I have to wait for two buses just to get here. It takes hours. You know, I don't think many people want to have this sickness."[12]

Many strenuously object to detaining ill people because of the possibly dangerous precedent it sets. If TB patients are locked away for treatment, might the concept of enforced care be extended unfairly to other individuals who pose far less of a public health risk?

Those who object point out how in recent years AIDS patients have often been victimized through unfair apartment evictions, job discrimination, and denial of health and life insurance benefits. Jeffrey Levi, a lobbyist for the Washington-based AIDS Action Council, summed up the troubling prospect when he said, "This is our greatest nightmare. Tuberculosis provides a handy excuse for people to do with AIDS patients what they have always wanted to do. Get rid of them completely. Move them to a locked airport or jail."[13]

But even if detaining TB patients for medical care could be morally and ethically justified, there would still be legal problems to contend with. Most of the present state laws permitting medical incarceration allow the person to be held only while he is still infectious. Then the individual is sent home with a prescription and instructions as to how to take his medication.

If the patient fails to complete his treatment on his own, he can become infectious again, and this time it might be with a drug-resistant strain of the disease. According to one physician who has treated numerous people with TB, "We give a patient four or five bottles of pills and wish him good luck. It would be amazing if they stayed on treatment until cured."[14] In response, some jurisdictions have passed recent legislation permitting the detention of TB patients until they've completed treatment. But most areas are still trying to strike a balance between safeguarding personal freedom and protecting the community.

Some public health officials have devised new strategies for effective long-term outpatient management. One viable alternative is known as Directly Observed Therapy, or DOT. In a DOT program someone actually watches as the patient swallows his daily medication. DOT programs can take a number of forms. For example, a nurse could administer the patient's medication by either going to the patient's home or having a field worker bring the patient to a clinic. To encourage a patient to continue to come in for treatment on his own, an assortment of incentives might be offered. These could include free hot lunches, food coupons, store vouchers, and in some cases even cash payments.

While financial incentives, or "bribes," amount to only a fraction of the cost of hospitalization, some people still feel it's wrong to pay a person to take the medication that could save his life. When doctors and nurses were asked at a TB seminar whether they agreed with paying tuberculosis patients twenty dollars a day to take their medication and a hundred dollars upon com-

A California health care worker visits a patient's home to administer Directly Observed Therapy (DOT).

pleting treatment, the majority of these health care professionals said no.

Yet others feel that the punitive quality of detained treatment has no place in health care. As the director of a major city's Bureau of TB Control commented, "There have been calls to quarantine patients or lock them up. I know there will be more, because when people are scared they grab for a simple answer. And locking sick people away is a simple answer. Simple, quick, and wrong."[15]

Perhaps the ultimate answer lies in a combination of solutions, which would include revamping a health care system that does not provide adequate services for the poor and disenfranchised. But regardless of the strategies targeted, immediate action is crucial. The battle against TB can still be won if we as a society act now.

APPENDIX: FOR FURTHER INFORMATION

The following groups are among the members of the National Coalition to Eliminate Tuberculosis:

AIDS Action Council
1875 Connecticut Avenue, N.W., Suite 700
Washington, DC 20009

American Association for Respiratory Care
11030 Ables Lane
Dallas, TX 75229

American Association for World Health
1129 20th Street N.W., Suite 400
Washington, DC 20036

American College of Chest Physicians
3300 Dundee Road
Northbrook, Illinois 60062-2348

American College of International Physicians
711 Second Street, N.E., Suite 200
Washington, DC 20002

American Geriatrics Society
770 Lexington Avenue, Suite 300
New York, NY 10021

American Health Care Association
1201 L Street, N.W.
Washington, DC 20005

American Hospital Association
840 North Lake Shore Drive
Chicago, IL 60611

American Jail Association
2053 Day Road, Suite 100
Hagerstown, MD 21740-9795

American Lung Association
1740 Broadway
New York, NY 10019-4374

American Public Health Association
1015 15th Street, N.W.
Washington, DC 20005

American Society for Microbiology
1325 Massachusetts Avenue, N.W.
Washington, DC 20005

American Society of Law, Medicine and Ethics
765 Commonwealth Avenue, 16th Floor
Boston, MA 02215

American Thoracic Society
1740 Broadway
New York, NY 10019-4374

Asian American Health Forum
116 New Montgomery Street, Suite 531
San Francisco, CA 94105

Association for Practitioners in Infection Control
1016 16th Street, N.W., 6th Floor
Washington, D.C. 20036

Association of State and Territorial
Health Officials
415 Second Street, N.E., Suite 200
Washington, DC 20002

Centers for Disease Control and Prevention
1600 Clifton Road, N.E.
Mail Stop E-10
Atlanta, GA 30333

College of American Pathologists
325 Waukegan Road
Northfield, IL 60093-2750

Department of Veterans Affairs
Office of Geriatrics and Extended Care (114)
810 Vermont Avenue, N.W.
Washington, DC 20420

Food and Drug Administration
5600 Fishers Lane
HFD 530 (NLRC)
Rockville, MD 20857

Health Resources & Services Administration
5600 Fishers Lane, Room 11-03
Rockville, MD 20857

Indian Health Service
5600 Fishers Lane, Room 6-05
Rockville, MD 20857

Infectious Diseases Society of America
Yale University School of Medicine
333 Cedar Street, 201 LCI
New Haven, CT 06510-8056

Migrant Clinicians Network
2512 South 1H 35, Suite 220
Austin, TX 78704

National Association of Community
Health Centers
1330 New Hampshire Avenue, N.W., Suite 122
Washington, DC 20036

National Association of County Health
Centers, Inc.
440 First Street, N.W., Suite 500
Washington, DC 20001

National Association of Hispanic Nurses
1501 16th Street, N.W.
Washington, DC 20036

National Black Nurses Association
1012 Tenth Street, N.W.
Washington, DC 20001-4492

National Coalition for the Homeless
1612 K Street, N.W., Suite 1004
Washington, DC 20006

National Coalition of Hispanic Health and
Human Services Organizations (COSSMHO)
1501 16th Street, N.W.
Washington, DC 20036

National Commission on Correctional
Health Care
2105 North Southport, Suite 200
Chicago, IL 60614-4017

National Foundation for Infectious Diseases
4733 Bethesda Avenue, Suite 750
Bethesda, MD 20814

National Health Care for the Homeless Council
P.O. Box 68019
Nashville, TN 37206-8019

National Heart, Lung and Blood Institute (NHLBI)
National Institutes of Health
9000 Rockville Pike
Building 31, Room 5A52
Bethesda, MD 20892

National Institute of Allergy and
Infectious Diseases (NIAID)
National Institutes of Health
9000 Rockville Pike
Building 31, Room 7A03
Bethesda, MD 20892

National Leadership Coalition on AIDS
1730 M Street, N.W., Suite 905
Washington, DC 20036

National Migrant Resource Program
1515 Capital of Texas Highway S., Suite 220
Austin, TX 78746

National Minority AIDS Council
300 Eye Street, N.E., Suite 400
Washington, DC 20002

National Public Health Information Coalition
P.O. Box 941804
Atlanta, GA 30341-0804

National Rural Health Association
301 East Armour Boulevard, Suite 420
Kansas City, MI 64111

National Urban League
500 East 62nd Street
New York, NY 10021

National Women's Health Network
1325 G Street, N.W.
Washington, DC 20005

New York Academy of Medicine
Two East 103rd Street
New York, NY 10128

New York City Department of Health
125 Worth Street, Room 331
New York, NY 10013

Office of Minority Health
5515 Security Lane, Suite 1000
Rockville, MD 20852

Pharmaceutical Manufacturers Association
1100 15th Street, N.W., Suite 900
Washington, DC 20005

Society for Hospital Epidemiology of America
875 Kings Highway, Suite 200
West Deptford, NJ 08096

Substance Abuse and Mental Health
Service Administration (SAMHSA)
5515 Security Lane
Rockwall II Building, Room 880
Rockville, MD 20852

Wasatch Homeless Health Care Program
404 South 400 West
Salt Lake City, UT 84101

SOURCE NOTES

CHAPTER 1

1. Paul Nunn and Kraig Klaught, "The Terrible Chest," *World Health*, July–August 1993, p. 28.

CHAPTER 2

1. Ken Chowder, "How TB Survived Its Own Death to Confront Us Again," *Smithsonian*, November 1991, p. 180.
2. "Brief History of an Age-Old Disease," *World Health*, July–August 1991, p. 22.
3. *Ibid.*
4. Mark Caldwell, *The Last Crusade: The War on Consumption* (New York: Atheneum, 1988), p. 42.
5. *Ibid.*
6. *Ibid.*, pp. 54–55.
7. Chowder, p. 188.
8. Caldwell, p. 192.
9. *Ibid.*

CHAPTER 3

1. Geoffrey Cowley, "A Deadly Return," *Newsweek* (March 16, 1992), p. 54.

2. Michael Specter, "Neglected for Years, TB Is Back with Strains that Can Be Deadlier," *The New York Times* (October 11, 1991), p. 44.
3. Philip J. Hilts, "Rise of TB Linked to a U.S. Failure," *The New York Times* (October 7, 1992), sec. B, p. 4.
4. Cowley, p. 58.
5. *Ibid.*
6. *Ibid.*
7. Sandra Friedland, "Waging War on Drug Resistant TB," *The New York Times* (May 10, 1992), p. 3.
8. Janice Hopkins Tanne, "Q & A About TB," *New York Magazine* (March 23, 1992), p. 34.
9. Elisabeth Rosenthal, "Doctors and Patients Are Pushed to Their Limits by Grim New TB," *The New York Times* (October 12, 1992), p. 1.
10. *Ibid.*

CHAPTER 4

1. "TB's Second Wave Claims 35% More Children," *The Star Ledger* (September 17, 1993), p. 15.

CHAPTER 5

1. Petra Graf and H.T. Chum, "Challenge in Tanzania," *World Health*, July–August 1992, 17.
2. "TB's Rise Tied to Travel and Public Complacency," *The Star Ledger*, November 15, 1993, 15.
3. *Ibid.*

CHAPTER 6

1. Mireya Navarro, "Far Away from the Crowded City, Tuberculosis Cases Increase," *The New York Times*, December 6, 1992, 49.
2. *Ibid.*

3. “Study Finds TB Danger Even in Low-Risk Groups,” *The New York Times*, October 18, 1992, 31.
4. Elisabeth Rosenthal, “TB Easily Transmitted, Adds a Peril to Medicine,” *The New York Times*, October 13, 1992, 1A.
5. *Ibid.*
6. *Ibid.*
7. *Ibid.*
8. *Ibid.*
9. *Ibid.*
10. Frank Ryan M.D., The Forgotten Plague: How the Battle Against Tuberculosis Was Won and Lost, (Boston: Little, Brown, 1992), 394.
11. Michael Specter, “TB Carriers See the Clash Between Liberty and Health,” *The New York Times*, October 14, 1992, B4.
12. *Ibid.*
13. Janice Hopkins Tanne, “Q & A About TB,” *New York*, March 23, 1992, 35.
14. Specter, *ibid.*
15. *Ibid.*

FOR FURTHER READING

BOOKS

Bates, Barbara. *Bargaining for Life: A Social History of Tuberculosis*. Philadelphia: University of Pennsylvania Press, 1992.

Caldwell, Mark. *The Last Crusade. The War on Consumption, 1862-1954*. New York: Atheneum, 1988.

King, Lester Snow. *Medical Thinking: A Historical Preface*. Princeton: Princeton University Press, 1982.

Myers, Arthur J. *Tuberculosis*. St. Louis, Missouri: Warren H. Green, 1970.

Ryan, Frank, M.D. *The Forgotten Plague: How the Battle Against Tuberculosis Was Won and Lost*. Boston: Little, Brown and Company, 1992.

Silverstein, Alvin. *Tuberculosis*. Hillside, N.J.: Enslow Publishers, 1994.

Taylor, Robert. *Saranac: America's Magic Mountain*. New York: Houghton Mifflin, 1986.

ARTICLES

Frandzel, Steve. "Drug-Resistant infections on the Rise," *Medical World News*, January 1993, p. 50.

Golub, Edward S. "Defeating Disease: Public Health Remedies vs. Biomedical Quick Fixes," *Omni*, September 1993, p. 4.

Groopman, Jerome. "T.B. or Not T.B? What to Do About a Plague," *New Republic*, March 8, 1993, p. 18.

"Increase in TB Cases Perils HIV-Positive," *Star Ledger*, November 17, 1992, p. 2.

Kilborn, Peter T. "Alarming Trends Among Workers: Surveys Find Clusters of TB Cases," *New York Times*, January 23, 1994, p. 1.

Porter, John, Keith McAdam, and Richard Feachem. "The Challenge Is International," *World Health*, July-August 1993, p. 13.

Rubel, Arthur J. and Linda C. Garro. "Social and Cultural Factors in the Successful Control of Tuberculosis," *Public Health Reports*, November-December 1992, p. 626.

"TB or Not TB?" *Consumer Reports*, September 1993, p. 580.

INDEX